PURPLE DAWN

Purple Dawn

Poems
by
EDWARD V. BONNER

Adelaide Books
New York / Lisbon
2019

PURPLE DAWN
Poems
By Edward V. Bonner

Copyright © by Edward V. Bonner
Cover design © 2019 Adelaide Books

Published by Adelaide Books, New York / Lisbon
adelaidebooks.org

Editor-in-Chief
Stevan V. Nikolic

All rights reserved. No part of this book may be reproduced in any manner whatsoever without written permission from the author except in the case of brief quotations embodied in critical articles and reviews.

For any information, please address Adelaide Books
at info@adelaidebooks.org
or write to:
Adelaide Books
244 Fifth Ave. Suite D27
New York, NY, 10001

ISBN: 978-1-951214-85-2

Printed in the United States of America

I would like to dedicate this work to my family, close friends, co-workers and all those who have believed and supported me.

Specifically, I would like to acknowledge my parents; Dennis and Rosemary. My wife Anna Marie; and my children Brooke Riley, Patrick Bonner.

*Thanks for the support and proof reading to—
Jocelyn Vaughan*

Thanks to Photo Editor Pixtr; Pexels.com; and Freestock Photos.com.

Contents

Preface *13*

Scream To Speak *15*

Body To Body *17*

Silver Threads *18*

Nine Innings *19*

In The Gloaming *20*

Waves Of Magic *21*

Lord's Butterfly *22*

Few Will Hear His Words *23*

Brushed With Love *25*

I Can't Stop *26*

Between Eternities *27*

Your Raptured Ways *28*

The Spirit Weeps *29*

Edward V. Bonner

A Tempting Glow **30**

God's Gift **31**

Life's Beauty **32**

Flaming Heart **33**

Light Of Tranquility **34**

Beyond The Stars **35**

Words **36**

Sun Succulent **37**

Eroding Melodies **38**

Mental Analysis **39**

Unbroken Whisper **40**

Saffron Blaze **41**

Trinket Of The Moon **42**

Minds Obscenity **43**

Beautiful Hands **44**

Love Simple **45**

Virginity **46**

To Look To The Sky **47**

Silken Skies **48**

Tangled Roots **49**

Take My Breath **50**

Heart Of Love **51**

Purple Dawn **52**

Unlaced Sweetness **54**

A Silent Journey **55**

The Way **56**

Let The Clouds Speak **57**

Morning Desires **58**

Capture The Moment **59**

A Place To Carry You Off **60**

Memories Endured **61**

Sorrowed Illusion **62**

Mystery Eyes **63**

I Was A Believer **64**

Ivory Darkness **65**

Black Butterfly **66**

Crimson Petal **67**

Water's Edge **68**

Your Naked Shadow   **69**

Verdant Whisper   **70**

Love Letter   **71**

I Love You   **72**

A Voice From The Sky   **74**

The Forest Breathes   **75**

I Loved Her, All Of Her   **76**

Wolves Of The Land   **77**

Run With The Wolves   **79**

Lover's Pilgrimage   **80**

Saturated Corners   **81**

Divine Stature   **82**

Captivated   **83**

Blossomed Thorn   **85**

Decaying Leaves   **87**

Open Waters   **89**

The Attic   **90**

Between Lives   **92**

Between Dreams   **93**

PURPLE DAWN

Natures Honor **94**

Masterpiece For Living **95**

Lower The Blinds **97**

Her Kiss Ripped My Heart **101**

Our Angel Is Flying **103**

A Little Girl With Wings **105**

Dear Love **106**

Meant To Be **107**

One Single Star **109**

My Visitor **110**

Radiant Flames **112**

About the Author **115**

Preface

To view into the heart. Poems reveal the internal thoughts of our lives. From future, present and past: The language moves the reader between reality and abstract thoughts of imagination.

We come face to face with happiness and heartbreak, conflict and suffering. "Love and shadow, love and goodness". We experience the meaning to the metaphor.

Scream To Speak

SCREAM TO SPEAK

How many secrets can you keep
While I sit in a cold laconic sleep
The forest nights I had to reap
Through a silent bog I hid so deep
From the raving wolves I hear and weep
Time my words I scream to speak
Listen here the cause I seek
I will run from you
To the highest peak

Lion
King of the beast
Power is his majesty
Royalty of their pride
Who carries great courage and strength
Hope is the lioness of the soul
A mother's love to guide and hold
She will never give up to protect her young
The hunter and the hunted is a will to survive

Body To Body

Locked outdoors in the bellowing snow
Icicles suspended from eaves
The sky was bright the mountains were white
The temperature far below

Body to body our heat will rise keeping the blood to flow
Blanketed arms that lavish our warmth
Hearts will surely know

Silver Threads

When love was all we had
Our dreams came true
Chasing what was our dream
Gave world to you
Our lips passed in the wind
As the flowery garden's fragrance sheds
Broken hearts will never mend
From thin silver threads

Nine Innings

When I thought I saw you in the stands
It made me feel faint and hollow inside
A tear dropped from my heart as this woman
turned and looked into my eyes
I had to look away for fear of losing you one more time
Your beautiful grace of the evening sun gave way
to my dreams through passionate rhymes
But every inning I had to glance
This woman of beauty seated near
Gave me one last chance
Oh the memory in the Laurels
Where we fell in love
A time of passion you dream of
The game has ended
What's the score
Was the home team winning
I was not sure
Nine innings of memories
This stranger has given
A breath from the stars of silent heaven

In The Gloaming

The winter wind blew
through the oak trees
In the soft rain you will
find a haze of ice crystals
scattered across the field
A spirit mist glows against
mountain's range
Where miracles come
alive in the gloaming to
the east
Time for lovers to embrace
where a
Breathless world of
enchanting mystery
Is held with contented
hearts

Waves Of Magic

I fell in love with a girl
Her name I shall not tell
Every day I dreamt our hearts would collide
Watching the sun go down in the mid summer's eve
I see her eyes aching inside

Irresistible waves of magic
Outpouring energy to the sky
Holding me close to her breast
Where our love shall never be denied

Lord's Butterfly

The earth is calm and cool
Your butterfly wings emerge and silently unfold

A metamorphosis transformation begins
to grasp the world within

They flutter in our moment of time
Flowers of the air, they show their beautiful design

Loving and free to see
You spread the Lord's beauty for me

Few Will Hear His Words

What thou find in a poor man's wallet
An amazing talent
To survive
Holding true to God's word
A secret for this man to cuddle on a doorstep
To wake in the morning
And breathe
Does he wonder about his next meal
Of course not
Food will come to him
At one time this man had a mother and father
Who fed and clothed him
Taught him their ways
To be a good person
And things will come
Every morning he walked to church and said his prayers
Not for himself

Edward V. Bonner

But for this world
A world peace
Unknown to billions of people
Only few will hear his words
And they will remember
The name of the Father, Son and Holy Spirit
Amen

Brushed With Love

Woman of my soul in sheer woven velvet
Knotted with lace that brushed her skin like falling rose petals
A timeless and romantic fragrance following her every move
Captured beauty beyond the northern hemisphere
Shy as I was
I embraced what love has made
Walking through this endless garden of euphoria
What breathtaking gem she holds to her blossom of eternity
Her elegant posture turned to me
Encompassing an aura of such beauteous art
You've taken me to paradise

I Can't Stop

I didn't know how to love
I ignored the truth
The pain changed me forever
Like a broken flower
Who ruled my spirit
Petals will fall to the earth
Ending a cycle
In the silent night

Between Eternities

If I wrote you a letter asking how much I mean to you
Will you answer
For
Our eternal torch is burning
An everlasting love revealed
A relentless yearning
Of few secrets concealed
Yet
Your eyes are hidden by a veil
With a luminous mist
Circling
A prevalent glow of amber
That will always exist
Then
I fall into a trance of your perfumed scent
Between eternities
Filling my heart content
Through my extremities

Your Raptured Ways

I am the one that was made of fun
Slow at wits and eaten to bits

The one who would dream of the sun
Where your life would become undone

Then one day you filled my heart with kerosene
Where I learned how people can be mean

Unspeakable regards of a human life
Your raptured ways were a dreadful plight

Don't ask don't tell for the pain I endured
In written words they are finally secured

The Spirit Weeps

Last night I watched myself sleep
Looking out I see
Your judgment is how the spirit weeps

People that fabricate are fools
Who corrupt and break the rules

Where beauty and pleasure seldom fail
Truth and reconciliation will always prevail

A Tempting Glow

You are the one I hear that sprouts wings
A voice in the clouds of beauty that sings

The skills of love
You hide from the show
Your crystal clear lips are a tempting glow

Reach out to my world of imagination
The kind of love
I want
Like an hallucination

Where I seek to unlock her treasure
I forego the path of pleasure

God's Gift

How I peer through the trees of the dead leaves falling
Keenly as my eyes shift from the left to right
Beyond the stagnant structures
And rotten smell of decay
What may be calm to the human ear
Is a city of wildlife in their own world
Each animal represents the true meaning of God's gift
How fortunate I am to see working,
feeding, playing of the wild
In their habitat
No moats
No bars
No glass
Free willing animals on their own
To survive a world
That is being destroyed by humans
What is
Is becoming small
What was
Is a memory of God's gift

Life's Beauty

I felt a tear holding wisdom to my heart
You came to me unseen from your visionary art

A lover's universe which captures the spirit of eternity
And live life's beauty in harmony

Where you lay in flavored spice
What love held
Unlaced passion in mystic paradise

Flaming Heart

Her lips of taste were so divine
Gave reason to heart
I held in mine

Woman of silence
I state to you
Beyond your spirit
Our time is new

Be still my queen
You are my flame
The fire within
My heart's to blame

Tomorrow is hope
A dreamer's way
Our pairing of love
For we shall stay

Light Of Tranquility

We are the windows of light
A journey for souls to make
right

The sun shines through to warm our hearts
We pray our love never parts

Wondering pearl your beauty is bright
You glow during the day and all through the night

A wisdom of knowledge deep in your mind
Showing love for true mankind

Beyond The Stars

Somewhere in the night
I wanted your love next to me
Tasting your body under candlelight,
you and I will live in ecstasy
Lost in your soul
Your heart will reign out of control
When we make love
Our enchanted minds will take us far beyond the stars
Past Saturn, Jupiter and Mars
Unlocking dreams that never existed
Kissing you knees to thighs as you persisted
Open up as you hold on to me
Oh my
The perfume of luxury

Words

Selective words can be misunderstood that
disseminate the mind of doubt

Fear within our heart will cause an
emotional response to shout

As life is impossible to be perfect
Do what is possible rather than regret

Eventually
Expectations of infallible vocabulary will be progressively met

Sun Succulent

Submerged in the grass
Drowning in the molasses
Of
The sky whispering by
With a contented sigh
The
Sun succulent
It's promise spent
On
Urgent vignettes
Without epithets

By Jocelyn Vaughan

Eroding Melodies

I dare not beg for one last smile
The demons rest in their insidious guile

For I am lured to a ghastly test
Within my tremulous pain,
I solely express

Eroding melodies; rewording charm
I fight to keep this man from harm

Let the winds howl, fulminate, rave!
Protecting him from entering a deserted passing grave

Embrace the shadow, bind with chains
Endure the power where righteous reigns!

Mental Analysis

Our emotional sensations are undefined
Conceivably distinguished by the eyes of the blind

Cast what shadows the mind's complexity
Erasing the worlds deliberate simplicity

Your internal scars hold their thoughts
Filtering through our endless knots

In the deepest part of the brain
We explore the heart of selfish shame

Unbroken Whisper

You and I together for one moment
Was a breadth measured in how life was chosen

Together our hearts were opened
When countless words were spoken

Our eyes whispered unbroken rhymes
Believing a wonderment love in time

Which holds a distance between impossible worlds
Manifest beyond the path of pearls

Saffron Blaze

Where bodies melt in a saffron blaze
Love's possession held an intense gaze

Satin laced and silver pinned
Her white milky layer dissolved into his lustrous skin

A deep journey from her shoulders to his lips
Clasped what naked souls will feed in a full eclipse

Trinket Of The Moon

Awakening dreams were made to come true
Her curls could dusk in the midnight dew

Far in the heavens the galaxies converge
Layers her heart of spontaneous surge

Unfolding the pleasures that she'll pursue
Immortalized wonders of bountiful and blue

To embrace the trinket of the moon's delight
Illuminates her beauty through the night

Minds Obscenity

Ripping in the twilight bog
Caged in emptiness of a misty fog

Your light wraps around me in mortal haze
Filled with ice running through my veins

In the depth of your tormented stay
A frost burnt mind of reality and reasoning, is
scratching and clawing looking for the "Way"

Through the mind's obscenity
We search the "Way"
Formulating propositions, following
a path of an internal enemy

Beautiful Hands

Rarely seen, is a special appeal
"The Way" of my soul is one-self you feel

Beginning in calmness, an ebbing flow
With the changing of winds, become
a tempest unknown

Beautiful hands are a vestige of forms
Absorbing the waves, winds and storms

When the powers of life is a thunder's dead
Returning to tranquility is honorably lead

Love Simple

The smallest things you miss
when you lose a lover
Are the simplest things you shared in life
A gaze into their eyes
A soothing kiss
The holding of a hand
Will follow you
Until the day you die

Virginity

Innocent of guilt she fell into a trance
Beyond the begging of angels
She lost her chance

Fate of virginity is absent from the mind
Diligently trying she fail with time

Her flower of heart holds her pain inside
With respect of her soul she must confide

To Look To The Sky

Poised on the edge of a stone bronzed peak
Where the wolves howled in a deafening shriek

Searching the night-glow for scattered pearls
We look to the sky, honoring the divine world

Wing of feathers, near silent flight
Absorbing noise, the owl sings at night

Where lives reach the midnight sun
Your humbled ways bred the essence of one

Silken Skies

Fluttered memories, blinded him still
Of jeweled diamonds and Tahitian pearls

An erotic touch to her black satin lips
Beauty the mystery in the moonlight eclipse

Her whispered words grasped the silken sky
With his poetic trance, it melted her thighs

Feeling the ecstasy that will appear
Awakened moments that shed his tear

Tangled Roots

Walking the trail of rising roots
Above and below we hobble in boots

Weathered from time of rain and shine
Tangled in silence along our line

Clusters and clumps, what
mushrooms are growing
Decaying and fermenting, the smell is exploding

A nip in the air, the breeze is soon near
From pine needles to rot, the nose can compare

It's a magic world that we understand
The reciprocal of life is in God's hand

Take My Breath

Take my breath when I awake
What's left of love, again we make

Before I moisten your tranquil lips
A taste of honey I can't resist

Unlace our dreams when angels sing
Bless the love that we may bring

Heart Of Love

It's okay to love some people and not know why
And never ask for love in return

Love with pain is a part of growing
Just another product of life

Unlace the temple of heaven's heart
Walk in spirit's innocence

Love is a big storm with the whole world drifting away
Ending up in prayer

Purple Dawn

When clouds dance
in a thunderstorm
He will hold you tight, and watch
the crystal angels take form

What thou cool wind blow from the north
Meet thou warm wind blow from the south

Fate for lovers do see
Two perfect souls will be

A bonded weeping willow
Flowing her tears through the meadow

With gale forces inseminate the seed.
Showering uncontrolled bursts of flowers
Turning and twitching a sky lighted tempest gathering power

Purple dawn to the red sunset blaze
Angels disappear in spring season haze

PURPLE DAWN

Most remembered in somber ways
Sprinkled light all through the day

Where buttercups bring sweetness fill
Calmness ends with earthen will

Unlaced Sweetness

Our glistening worlds we come to defy
A soften skin your spirit lies

Unclothed your body, such beauty revealed
Your flowered gate of flesh is sealed

White roads of heaven, a paradise we walk
Through a garden of eve, such intimate talk

Oh my love
My spirit is thee
A kingdom of dreams for you shall see

Beautiful beauty beyond the sun's rays
Shines down on your skin, as a milky haze

Your cover

Unlaced sweetness upon your breast
Provoking utmost desire and passion in light of rest

Come defy our love at ease
As joyful hearts we are to please

A Silent Journey

Under a breath of an angel
A whisper's word of charm
Your enchanted walk through the gardens
A silent journey in arms

Your exotic smell of perfume
Rushing through the air
Flowers of romance
All for us to share

Beyond the heavens atmosphere
A soul's midnight charm
A breathless kiss of magic
Will guard our love from harm

The Way

Fluidity adjusts to the objects.
Finds a way around or through.
To improve themselves we emulate a flowing energy.
Empty our mind.
Adapting and changing with life's complexities.
Shapeless like water until we fill our soul.
Let go the energy and reshape your mind.
Absorb waves, thunder and storms.
We follow the path of internal energy.
Your humbled ways breed the essence of one.

Let The Clouds Speak

The wind fell to his word.
Breathing in her thoughts and temptations heard.

She roamed the planet in beloved form.
Confronting rain and thunderous storms.

He whispered her name across the sea.
Brushed her skin over the eastern breeze.

Letting the clouds speak in many prophecies.
Her natural motion moved with tremendous velocity.

And where love has met a crying sigh.
Their tranquil ambience surrounded the sky.

Morning Desires

It was a dream inside
holding you tight
What magic in the air
turned to gold

The girl in the woods
whispered softly
Invisible words from a shallow breath

Our lips fused under the skyline of oak
Feeling your skin on my hands
You melted right through me

Acorns falling like raindrops
Covered the brittleness of the earth's debris

Making love between the fallen branches
We inhaled what our body senses

Capture The Moment

I sat in silence upon the forest hill,
my idled soul wrapped alone and still.

I hear a grouse drumming in display,
a crescendo of beats rapidly increasing its way.

Under a canopy of tangled vines,
lies a sweet succulent fruit intertwined.

Grapes are wild and abundant all around,
making easy pickings from the darkened ground.

A brown blur of feathers pummeling the air,
captures the moment in this social affair.

The quality of life is splendor.
Grasp and hold to your heart,
for nature's love is tender.

A Place To Carry You Off

I can understand how loneliness borders madness
You keep searching through your brain for answers
and it feels like walking through a maze of emptiness

When you look at the stars will they make me real again?
And when I see your face will you make me believe again?

Let us go to a place where acorns blanket the ground
Wild black berries with the sweetest taste are found

I want to lie here with you
I'm your writer
I am your dreamer

Let me carry you off to the forest
With beautiful passion and mystic rhymes
Unclothed bodies are frozen in time

Memories Endured

Following the moon's glimmering light,
the huntsman searched in the forest night.

Generously wise and fiercely determined,
flames in his soul were quietly burning.

He answered a call from his nightingale blue.
The clothes on her body were a sweet cotton too.

Salt caramel spice suffused the air,
sending shivers through his silver hair.

Secretly caressing,
pulsating pure,
what memories sweet they both endured.

Gliding, penetrating,
relentlessly entwined,
captures their bodies intensely enshrined.

Don't speak in the silent arms of the moonlight,
until you dance to the shining stars at midnight.

Sorrowed Illusion

Crawling out from the rocks and shedding her skin,
summoning storms and a violent wind.

Watching in ruin from the shadowed ledge,
the jasmine wilts on the water's edge.

It's a madness to fall so deeply in love.
I was crazy to take the pain from above.

The sorrowed illusion which I then did feel.
The devil's own daughter has closed the deal.

Attention alone is what your soul craved.
Not being saved from a lustful day.

Leave what horror's that is stored for me.
I am your puppet, hung dry
from the black willow tree.

Mystery Eyes

The morning is full of clouds in the seasoned heat.
"My eyes are clear."

If the mystery is hidden within the shell,
without opening,
it will rot inside.

Summer comes after spring.
The withered leaves are gone.

Lovers moan in delight, fulfilling their dream.

With his semen deeply implanted in her womb.
Secrets are revealed from the petal flower.

A promise that they are one.
Joined together forever.
To what human beings cherish,
of truly being alive.

I Was A Believer

Tracing the stars each night our eyes met.
At dawn we kissed and made love.
We were beautiful undercover.
Boiling to the point of overflowing,
I fell in love with a girl miles away.

I did not know.
I couldn't find the words when you buried me without regret.
How blind and ignorant I was, chasing your cry.

I heard and I followed.
The pain you left will never go away.
I was a believer.

In due time I will be gone from tormenting I caused.

Ivory Darkness

Your inviting lips...a deep rich ruby hue,
plunged deep into my dreams.

Through tears,
a tint of brilliant madness slowly dissolved into my flesh.

Between laughter and despair, love was a mindful game.

Feeding the flames with my bones, was like
the burning sun crossing a desert.

Years of silence,
your pain was hidden in the depths of an aphotic sphere.

Then one day your circle opened up to the wind.
Ivory darkness fell to happiness.

Your shadow dissolved into light and a violet
splendor cast goodness upon your heart.

Black Butterfly

The night was made into madness.
To forget where we came from is like a distant
candle burning on the edge of the planet.
For the wolves to wake up from their sleep and
hunt prey completely devouring lust.
Truly beautiful to put into words, a wild beast trapped
in an unlocked cage clawing to get out, she is her own.
Letting her hang on the wall beside your
trophies would be prison of destruction.

Crimson Petal

She tempts her love in the night hours.
Whispering low, drawing him in.
Where does this tenderness come from?

Moments the glassy darkness holds, now slides
the crimson petal cradling a dove.

Enraptured by her surrounding warmth, he is
captivated by a more ravenous passion.

Speechless, he lies in waiting.

Water's Edge

Under a fading sunset,
gorgeous cascading waves whispered dreams to a small child.

On the water's edge stood poised the figure of an angel so
exquisitely formed, her shadow danced with the breeze.

Bewildered by this image, pure joy
enters the young lad's soul.
Questioning this angelic figure, "why are you here?"

The answer is quite simple, angels are
everywhere watching over us.

In the most mysterious ways, be the best of who you are.

Raindrops fall on sunny days for a reason.
Your guardian is near to you, protecting your heart.

Your Naked Shadow

Lost into the shadows,
I see your eyes watching every move.

A deepened breath, my heart beats a fury of flames.

What keeps me close is your taste.
A taste of your golden honey that will
make me scream for your hive.

A puzzle waiting to be solved,
your infinite lips are a naked passion
where I want to be torn apart.

Your rose tattooed skin beautifies madness
and protection against love.

Influencing man's weakness, your tailored
body beams reverend and strong.

I am here.
Your hidden desire.
An eternity,
you shall live forever.

Verdant Whisper

Verdant pine needles stir in the early breeze.

Birds sing
a resurrection of life.
Miracles fill the earth.

Tree buds bursting in the blue,
and the leafy blades begin to sprout.

Descending white and pink blossoms into the air.

Sitting by the lakeside watching the eagles soar.

The sun smiled back at me each morning I heard her whisper.

Earthen woman let your wild flowers bloom.

Passionate currents and water flow, a
silvery essence in the early glow.

Love Letter

North to south; east to west.
And every time I looked at you.
I whispered your name.
Precious one.
I hear the beauty in your words.
The love that is in your heart.
The mystery in your soul.
Like a collection of stars.
We will share the same sky
and breathe the same air.

I Love You

Powerful phrase
I love you
Unless you mean it
Don't ever say it
Many died from it
Many killed for it
Many suffered for it

Many see the Elysium
A room full of souls
Opening the door for them to endure

Of loneliness

When you truly mean
I love you
Happiness is deep in your heart
Togetherness never part

You give your life

PURPLE DAWN

What's yours and mine
A life of sharing
A life of caring
Children bearing

Traveling worlds
They carry their heart

I love you
Seeds the fire of burning desire

However, untrue love is an emptiness
Of fools leading to hopelessness

A Voice From The Sky

Your eyes rescued my heart.
And when you smiled,
you left me speechless.

We were alone,
I laid my head down.
A voice from an angel whispered in my ear,
asking me,
what is love?

I looked to the stars.
Cried your name.

Trying to hold back,
I couldn't fight.
I was scared to be alone.

On a oneway path,
we grew up apart.

Fate doesn't lie,
we keep coming back.

The Forest Breathes

Deep in the forest,
hemlocks surrounded by majestic beech,
white pine,
maple and chestnut.

Openings were few,
natural meadows and unmeasurable
mountain tops flourished unseen.

A calm redolent earth has given us respect where freedom
fills the soul of a man with peace of nature's wonder.

The forest breathes around you.
Listen to her call.
A muffled whisper through the changing leaves.

Rich in secrets,
hidden by earth.
A walking escape never before seen.
Ornaments from God,
sculpted for beauty.
A soothing gift to enjoy never to be destroyed.

I Loved Her, All Of Her

Covered with your scented oils,
you glided across my skin, intertwined with my body
like ravenous waves engulfed in raw passion.

Relax,
we have been starving.
It's not about dreams,
it's the endless depth of our soul.

My thirst craved your wet lips.
Your mouth on my mouth.
Revealing our nakedness,
my hands glanced your glistening breast.

A tapestry embroidered with hunger.
A longing woven into treasure.
A primal yearning:
quench my palate with your sweetness.

Love will make us remember.

Wolves Of The Land

When the moon breaks the mountain top,
the wolves sing to clear the sky.

Time is frozen from the sound of calling,
as their majesty guides the pack of glowing eyes.

Far from being a mob scene, the hunt
is masterfully coordinated.

Harmonious howls pierce the calm wind,
sending chills through the creatures of the night.

Under the symphony of collided spirits,
fractured bones are catapulted into the heavens.

Listening from a distance, you can hear an elk moan.
The sound is a blood curdling scream.

Wolves pounce with each breath, ripping the flesh.
The young watch this behavior and learn
how they can play the game.

Edward V. Bonner

Lip licking.
Growling.
Snarling of teeth.

Each member knows exactly their seat.

Ending a successful hunt.

The alpha male cares for his pride, so
the family can relax and feast.

Run With The Wolves

You are inspiring to the human mind,
what inspiration should be.
An invigorating spirit of light, holding out your flair.
As love and beauty decree.

A reverent life shouting out to share,
for what waiting does pass.
When we're alone, it's time to lay your hands
on my body, and let go of the past.

One hearts with thee, you are my skin.
Softness in glow, our love begins.

Oil's to preserve of lavender and coconut, a vanity we keep.
Run with the wolves before life passes, in our nocturnal sleep.
The wolves are human beings.

Lover's Pilgrimage

When you are not with your lover,
you are not in the presence.

On every trip,
there was only one objective,
to feel the innermost love lived in virtue.

Every syllable is truth.
To be in complete control of one's character.

Acknowledge each small gift that will ripen your splendor.

Embrace the fall wind and let it dance between bodies.

Unfold your heart,
follow the journey through a finite path.

Love is limited to death.
Accept your love as an echo,
a fading memory.

Saturated Corners

The dancing flames from the dusty
lantern in our tenement palace,
imitated our tongues
reaching for the saturated corners of our illicit bliss.

Divine Stature

Knowingly you destroyed a man's life.
Is this a secret or rare thing you live for pleasure?

Full of hate and laughter,
a breathing tick that feeds on sadness.

So many thanks for the hurting
and the condemnation that stained his world.

The glamorous demand of your social
status for immediate attention,
all combined the deliverance for a divine stature.

Tearing someone apart until there's nothing
but shreds for the devil's flames,
you laugh with cynical manipulation.

Captivated

For many, there is only silence.
However,
tell yourself it won't kill your dreams.
She knew he lived in the closet.
For years she lived a life of celibacy.

Honoring a commitment to her marriage,
she remained true to her family.

Miles away,
A gentleman from her hometown
had a tremendous ambition in life.
Dreams to build and places to go…

However,
His married life of loneliness,
was killed by an overdraft and overdrawn spouse.
A collision fractured his mind.

Moving his little bit of life,
the calling was answered.

Edward V. Bonner

"Forty years ago she passed my desk with
a smile. Why didn't we talk"

The wind blows hard and cold in mid. January.
Much of the green grass was covered with snow.
All the birds and animals were quietly
hiding in trees and underbrush.

There is a place in that lonely heart that will never be filled,
but will drive a person mad with obsession.

"One call"
"Just one call"
Were all they needed.

To hear another one's voice with passion,
captivated Romeo and Juliet's soul.

Blossomed Thorn

Like a bud-less tree seeking sustenance
in a fertile land for rain,
he pleaded for love.
Found amongst the sheath,
thorns spewed out raw unheard of dialect.

His story held meaning.
Unbeknown,
the knot from her lace began to tighten.

The bedroom began to spin.
Vodka and Red Bull was his enemy…
"A mixture eminent for destruction"

After a smoke
she returned.
Upon this earth he vacated reason.
They made love.

The bedroom…
The laughter…

Edward V. Bonner

The dancing…
"All a "FKN" mind playing games"

It was real to him.
A getaway for her…

Her circle was breaking free.
His was caving in.

Like a rapist on the street,
"hell" was coming early.
Only he didn't know.

Truly his love poems inspired what passion was left.
Depth is hidden in the forest,
but the curvature of the earth is seen from space.

Lying in bed,
the leaves turned dry and brittle.
Everything turns to dirt.

The drunken bee's sting!
Her earrings are left on the table.
Spin to win.
Feel her disease.
It was only yesterday.
Balance is somewhere.
He believed.

Decaying Leaves

I miss the confusion
The meaning
Just as I knew misery
I sweat nervously gazing out the window

I see
Laying on a hedge
a mantis with her triangular head
and bulging eyes
praying with arms folded
waiting for a victim

Am I this victim
Where her smile feeds me
to stay alive

Arms wrapped around my waist
Unspoken, delicate, and on the edge
I cannot run away

Edward V. Bonner

Curse this feeling
To believe
What is there to believe
I have forgotten
But I keep going
And going

I love you
I do hate you
I ignore the pain

The sun pans across the sky
Darkness sets in
I am a prisoner of decaying leaves
waiting for the moon to rise

Open Waters

Seeking the endless fruit
in uncharted waters,
expelling my lungs,
I excused life's identity
from the words of your mouth.

My drunkenness for passion
was the pleasure of death,
trying to imagine
you with a tender breath.

And when you are alone,
call me sometime,
to hear the contentment
in my life,
rain or shine.

I hope ending up like you,
having life figured out.

The Attic

Up the creaky stained dried attic stairs.
Hidden words become a dreamer's delight.

A single forty watt incandescent bulb emits a three-dimensional shadow, only the bravest human will investigate.

Dust particles float between the sun's rays and the dark abyss.
Unpublished covert files,
tablets,
binders and literature,
a forgotten maker of reality.

Boxes full of things we might need,
pots and pans, antique glass ware, clothing.
Games like Monopoly, Parcheesi and checkers.
All waiting to come out of hibernation.

Even a good few strands of silk gathered
spider webs hang from the rafters.

PURPLE DAWN

Only to give us a miniature tantrum
when they cling to our face.

Swatting, batting and slashing away the sticky goo,
crying out the spider may be crawling on you.

Finally reaching the lone cedar chest.
Positioned in the middle of the room.

I see the past,
I see the present.
I see the future.

Everything is connected,
all part of a whole.

Life is full of ups and downs for us to understand.
Our choice is to follow.

Between Lives

Because life matters, not everything can be.
The body begins to formulate an understanding where
there is no measurable distance between space.

Becoming still is an indifference the mind will not travel.
Counting is to understand a beginning,
where a lifestyle is to prosper from imagination.

The stars that pass through the night are like
an endless forest hidden with creation.
The womb of the universe,
is the creation which leads' life to all that is.

Love is the essence clothed in hands of enlightenment.
We shall live to face the spirit of existence
and what we understand about flesh,
is what we are struck down with.

And now the stars bloom gorgeously away from our hand.

Between Dreams

I can't change who I am.
I don't know where to begin.

Gazing from the highest cliff,
a beautiful dove called from afar.
Her amber eyes blurred the
universe with endless passion.

Between dreams
and reality
I breathed into her soul.

When you said the words to me,
you stole my heart.
Happiness traveled beyond the oceans,
above the mountains and through the valleys.
I could not resist the tenderness that
overwhelmed my fragile loneliness.

A piece of my heart was stolen,
leaving the arrow broken,
as you slowly pulled
the remains out,
I have bled till this day.

Natures Honor

The sun and the moon venture to find their
God wrapped around the wavering clouds.
Shadows appear across the Rocky Mountains.

A faint howl is heard through the misty evergreens.
Like a child reaching out from a deep slumber,
the wolf spirit calls to the souls of the past.

Unyielding laws hover for survival,
yet his poetic love calms his ferocious path with society.

Save the code.
Invite life and
honor her beauty.

I am you.
We are one.

Masterpiece For Living

Without words, depth conceives magic.
Igniting power we encourage victory above the horizon.

Peace is the splendor of elegant smiles.
He who binds the earth from joy, spreads pain to its people.

However, laughing needs but little.
Perhaps an honorable thought of compassion or gratitude.

Funny is funny.
Laughter expresses a portrait to every human personality.
It will cross boundaries that separate people.
A spontaneous uncontrollable emotion, randomly
unexpected thoughts like capturing a blooming daffodil.
Cause and affect.

Where there's nothing to give, laughter opens
doors to a symphony of chords.
A simple masterpiece promoting creativity
to the minds of young and old.

Edward V. Bonner

Day or night, when it's raining or bright.
Giggles.
Smiles and explosive roars.
This art we carry embraces scores.

Lower The Blinds

A faint murmured word spoken with a stunning smile.

Like opening your eyes in the early morning
and gazing at Jupiter all alone.
A surreal glow filled the heavens from her beauty.
An enchanting fragrance, sweet -
scented Dior Hypnotic Poison
relaxed a tense mood and eased my heart.

Within the captured secrets that held myself,
I kissed her warm lips.
A tender touch of breath brushed against her body.
Gliding the curvature of her breasts
under an ivory laced poet blouse,
unbound words blossomed.

We walked to my room and stood at the door hypnotized.
Her image emanates unimaginable gracefulness.
"I want you here tonight"
In a desired silence I revealed.

Edward V. Bonner

Unlocking the door,
we held each other like the god Helios embracing the earth.

Thoughts wreathed our emotions.
I whispered looking into her eyes.
"I want to dance"
Our dance.
Together.
Alone.

Reasons
by Earth Wind and Fire.
Why I love you
I can't find the reason.

In our romantic world we danced until
passion breathed into our bodies.

"Mountains over mountains.
The nights we stood outside staring at the North Star,
imagining our eyes will meet again."

Now.
This moment.
What I am to you is real.
Then again we kissed.

Without breaking our rhythm, I carried her to bed.

PURPLE DAWN

Legs wrapped around my waist.
Window blinds lowered with only a filtered cast
radiant enough I could see her splendor.

Another soft kiss on her neck,
earlobes and shoulders.
She wanted more.

Removing her blouse.
Tracing her breasts, feeling her tighten between my fingers.
Closing her eyes she gasped arching back.

Slowly kissing and licking.
Tongue tipped pirouette around,
to the sides and under.
Lead an integrating a tease.

Let it storm.

All our instincts crystallized
into a silent adoration.
I succumbed to her beauty.

I removed my shirt, and then, our skin met.
Cold becomes warm.
Warm becomes wet.

The excitement intensifies.

Edward V. Bonner

My lips followed her scent down to her thighs.
Guiding my head.
Pulling me in.
She was unstoppable.
I was unstoppable.

But a kiss is what I craved.
Warmth I desired.
This wasn't only ecstasy, this was lost love.
So beautifully nude,
we made love.

Having her fall asleep into my arms,
I closed my eyes and drifted away.
I surrendered my soul,
till the end of time.

Her Kiss Ripped My Heart

This was all she
knew
I rode her star to the
moon

It was late at
night
The heaven's eyes where
bright

A call that broke my
soul
Passion threw her blood
in-control

It was a silent wintry
blur
Secrets finally fell
upon the breast of
hers

Edward V. Bonner

And what I risked
Someone I could turn to and
kiss

It was all a game of laughter and
fun
The poems I wrote fell hard from the
sun

When I needed her the most
she let me
down

I sliced my wrist and fell to the
ground

I wasn't the person that
fits
Something like
this

Finally the spirits are taking
advice

Our Angel Is Flying

Life's journey through adventure
and love spreads comfort
to the mind of a dreamer.

From time to eternity,
her words gave wisdom
to the soul.

Lessons upon lessons,
her garden is filled
with love stories,
nature and tears.

Reaching out to the world,
poetry
soothed the body
while enriching the heart.

People love to see a rainbow
etched across sky.

Edward V. Bonner

Jocelyn's poems
touched each and every one
differently.
What forms is a prism of colors
sprinkled in the atmosphere.
A rainbow of beauty.

Beyond the surface,
life has taught me
one of hardest
lessons to learn.

A Little Girl With Wings

Did you ever notice a weed
growing out of a crack
from your driveway?
A lone bud that grows
unnoticed from this weed
becomes a flower.

Did you ever find
a wild strawberry plant
in the middle of the forest?
A vibrant beauty
growing from the dark soil.

It takes a lot to breathe
and understand this world.
God has this special way for
us to learn why we exist.

A little girl with wings scatters her gifts.
A lone red cardinal sings to your heart's content.

They all require sacrifice.
Why are you afraid?

Dear Love

Dear love,
it began under the stars.
The white mountains reached for the clouds.
The heavens captured the galaxy.
That's when I walked away from this merciless realm.

The winter freeze.
The summer heat.
The late night talks.
We were one in two silent worlds.
Yet we where under the same moon
and every clear night we spoke with our eyes.

Will you sing with me?
Play the night as if it's our last.
Will you dance with me?
So I can hold you close before we pass.

What became of my weak soul that needed love?
An arrow affixed with a broken heart,
fell once again.

Meant To Be

I fell in love
with the stars
that twinkle in her eyes

A place where the ferns
whispered secrets to the wind
and bend the moon
across the sky

I fell in love
with her satin lips
One evening in the park
under a pine
we finally kissed

Auburn hair flowing
from her shoulders
Leaves swirling in the wind
To touch
To feel

Edward V. Bonner

Her gentle grace
I was falling on teardrops
when we embraced

Love
Ignites fantasy
to fulfillment of reality

The hardest part in life
Is to never know
if
it was meant to be

One Single Star

Can I get to know your thoughts
Take it slow and we can be beautiful
If you're lonely don't worry
I'll be here to listen

Call my name
Let me see where your heart exists
We can cast out the viscous world
One single star will listen to our words

Friendship will bloom through a golden rose
Something we can turn to
Where we will last forever

We will never have to wish upon

My Visitor

I wish I knew
I've been waiting
Another day
Alone again

I saw it on her face
What could we do
Why didn't I listen

Read "White Fang"
Together we can analyze
Investigate and debate

Above the summit
Through the Alleghenies
Pressing upon the minds of two lovers
An unending vastness crushed upon two hearts

A faint giggle
rose with the thermals
amidst the maples and oaks

It was her voice
that soared into the heavens

PURPLE DAWN

Days later
Asking for help
I glanced out the window
A lone red cardinal fixated
Eye to eye

Tranquility and peacefulness
melted my heart
A messenger
A spirit
answering my cry

You are an angel surrounding
me with love
You give me peace
Knowing you are in peace
I love you
Always

Radiant Flames

The shifting currents
shoulder the cerebral coast,
sending sediment
through your brain.
Instinctively the mind wakes
more quickly to agony,
than a star-shaped heart
radiant with flames.

Brushing silica
from your fingers...
Scars of persuasion
like a violent storm.
The darkened skies
behind your lidded eyes
wild with wind
and beautifully formed.

This field wields it's bouquet:
hypnotic, exotic and consuming.
Our bodies tossed on thick moss,
surrender in kudzu,
soaked with sweat.
Too late to understand,
fate was in our hands.

Thanks to co-author Jocelyn Vaughan

Jocelyn Vaughan

October 11, 1961 - May 20, 2018
She lives on through her poetry,
our memories and hearts.

About the Author

The titles of Edward V. Bonner's poetry, suggests some ways in which the poems inside balance the universe. Most of the poems examine the themes of beauty and risk, pleasure and danger, in the context of one of three kinds of relationships: to romantic partners, to the spiritual world, and to the world of nature. But while these concerns are shared by much of humanity, Bonner's poems sound consistently personal.

As a young child, Ed grew up in a rough area of Pittsburgh Pennsylvania, a small mill town called Hazelwood. Raised by his mother and grandparents until the age of 13. (As Edward Fromen) His mother remarried. At 15 years old he was adopted by his stepfather.

Growing up Bonner got into trouble like most city kids. Only he was the lucky one. An avid outdoorsman
6th degree black belt in Shotokan karate
Holds an Associate degree in business
Holds aeronautics degree and a A&P license.
Author of "**One Kiss- Just One Kiss**"
Author of "**Through the Eyes of a Lost Boy**"
Published in "Adelaide" literary magazine (**Purple Dawn**) Year III Number 11, January 2018.
Published in "Adelaide" literary magazine
(**Beyond the Heavens**) Year III Number14, July 2018.
Finalist: ADELAIDE VOICES LITERARY CONTEST 2018 "**Verdant Whisper**".

www.ingramcontent.com/pod-product-compliance
Lightning Source LLC
Chambersburg PA
CBHW032235080426
42735CB00008B/869